# Little Joey's Sunshine Adventure

place picture

THIS BOOK BELONGS TO

_____

# Little Joey's Sunshine Adventure

Written By Lisa Jude Cellucci

Illustrated By Marc Tedesco

Text © 2016 Lisa Jude Cellucci
Illustrations © 2016 Marc Tedesco
All rights reserved. No portion of this book may be reproduced in whole or in part without written permission from Lisa Jude Cellucci, with the exception of brief excerpts in reviews. For information regarding permission, contact Lisa at LTLC219@aol.com.

Published in The United States

**Little Joey's Sunshine Adventure**
Written by Lisa Jude Cellucci
Illustrated by Marc Tedesco

Summary:
A young boy's relationship with his grandfather inspires him to go on an adventure, where he makes new friends and learns a valuable lesson.

ISBN 978-1533120120

1. Adventure   2. Family/Friendship   3. Life Lessons   4. Curiosity   5. Animals

Book and Cover Design by Christie Colangione-B

Printed in The United States of America
1 2 3 4 5 6 7 8 9 10

First Edition

Produced in 2016 in association with
Badavino Creative Studios
**Badavino Creative Studios website address: jimmybadavino.com**

I would like to dedicate this book to my husband, Rich, for his unwavering support and never ending belief in my dreams. Also, to our beautiful daughter, Gabriella, who is our greatest creation, and my strongest inspiration. I love you both.

I would also like to acknowledge those family and friends whose love and support has helped me along my journey.

A special thank you to Tricia, whose help from heaven made this book possible.

~Lisa Jude

Hi, my name is Joey. Everyone calls me 'Little Joey'. Mom and Dad say that I ask a lot of questions. "But, that's okay," they say. "That's how you learn."

I have a grandpa who I love very much, and I know he loves me too!
I like to sit on his lap and listen to his stories about when he was little like me. He likes to teach me all sorts of interesting things.

My grandpa is so smart!

Grandpa always tells me that life is not always about the end result, but how we get there that counts. I didn't understand what Grandpa meant by this until I went on my sunshine adventure.

What's a sunshine adventure you ask?
Well, let me tell you about it.....

One day while I was playing outside, the sun was starting to set. It was getting late, and I was called home to take a bath and have dinner. That meant no more fun for the day, and I was mad!

I made up my mind right then and there that I was going to find out what happens to the sun when it sets. Why does it have to spoil all of my fun?

Why does it sting my eyes in the morning when it wakes me up?

I decided this was the day. After dinner and a bath, I asked my parents if I could go on a sunshine adventure. My mom said, "As long as you stay in our back yard, you may."
Dad helped me make snacks and pack my sleeping bag for my adventure.

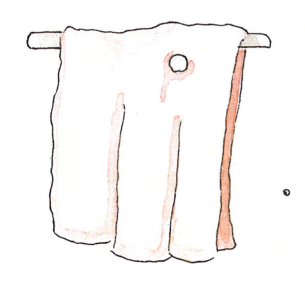

By the time I headed for our back door, the sun was already setting. I had to hurry. As I walked into the yard, I was greeted by a small, brown bunny. I asked the bunny, "Do you know what happens to the sun when it sets?"

The bunny twitched her pink nose,
thumped her soft little foot, and replied,
"I never thought about it much. I'm not sure."

"Would you like to find out?" I asked her.
"Sure", said the bunny. "Why not?"

We walked a little further and happened across a pretty, polka dotted deer.

"Hi," said the deer. "Where are you two going?"

"We're going on a sunshine adventure. Would you like to come?"

"What is that?" asked the deer.

"Well, we are trying to find out what happens to the sun when it sets."

"Oh, I would love to come along!" said the deer.

As we walked along, we chatted. We all were becoming good friends. The sun was getting lower and the sky was turning pretty shades of pink and orange. We noticed a beautiful bird flying above our heads. He was a cardinal. I asked him, "What are you doing up there?"

He replied, "Nothing special. Just flying."

"Perhaps you can be of help?" I asked. "Do you know what happens to the sun when it sets?"

"Not a clue," said the cardinal. "But I would love to find out."

Not far away, a nosey squirrel asked to join our happy group. "Sure," I said. "We could always use more company."

Grandpa always told me you can never have too many friends. He said, "Friend collecting is like collecting buttons. They are all different, they all come from somewhere that they were once connected to, and they all can be helpful at different times."

My friends and I were having such a good time on our adventure that we didn't realize how late it was. We laughed and laughed!

The sun was just a sliver of warmth in the now purple-blue sky. All of us were tired, and glad to see the sun start to go to sleep. We decided we would rest under an old oak tree.

I spread out my sleeping bag and shared my snacks with my new friends. They sat on the roots of the big tree, just like I sit on my grandpa's knee.

That's right! The big, tired sun finally set. However, my new friends and I had fallen asleep first.

The next thing I remember, I was waking up to the sun, greeting me with its warm rays. But this time I felt different about it. I wasn't angry, or confused, or curious.
I was happy!!!

Do you know why?...

...I looked around at all of my new friends, and realized something very important.

Sometimes it doesn't matter if we get all of our questions answered, like what happens to the sun when it sets, as long as we have friends to share it with when it rises.

THE END

Now I understand what Grandpa was trying to teach me. It is not always about the end results, but the journey we take and who we share it with.
I can't wait to get home to tell him what I learned, how much I love him, and how happy I am to journey with him.....

"I know my animal friends really don't talk, however, it made my adventure more exciting! My grandpa tells me I have a vivid imagination, and I think Grandpa does too!"

## Author Lisa Jude Cellucci

Lisa Jude Cellucci is a writer, artist, and homemaker, who resides in Troy, New York with her husband Rich, their daughter Gabriella, and their two dogs, Roo Roo and Ben. She attended the College of St. Rose in Albany, NY, where she studied Graphic Design and Elementary Education. She enjoys photography, cinema, antiquing, and spending time at the ocean.

Lisa is grateful for the love and support of her family and friends.

Look for more publications in the future by Lisa Jude.

## Illustrator Marc Tedesco

Marc Tedesco is an Illustrator and Graphic Design Artist. He has illustrated original artwork for the NBA franchise, including national commercials, and has conceptualized and designed art content for CBS sporting events. Marc is also an experienced freelance artist, and has his artwork displayed in restaurants, salons, and private residences. Marc has been recognized as a finalist in the 2016 Pro Max Awards for his illustrations, and currently works as a Graphic Design Artist at CBS Sports in New York City.

## In Memory

Lisa and Marc would like to dedicate this book in loving memory to their grandfather, Wallace Tedesco, with whom his likeness is represented in this book. Their inspiration came from his strength of character, integrity, morals, and most importantly, love for his family.

Thank you, Grandpa,

We love you,

Lisa Jude and Marc

## The Warming Sun

The early breeze the warming sun
Oh how I would love to be the morning sun
I would shine my warm rays on my family and friends
and laugh all day till the morning ends!

By Lisa Jude Cellucci

Made in the USA
Charleston, SC
08 September 2016